SEA SNAKES

Sierra Wilson

The World of Snakes

www.av2books.com

Step 1
Go to **www.av2books.com**

Step 2
Enter this unique code
CAVYMK7BL

Step 3
Explore your interactive eBook!

AV2 is optimized for use on any device

Your interactive eBook comes with...

Contents
Browse a live contents page to easily navigate through resources

Audio
Listen to sections of the book read aloud

Videos
Watch informative video clips

Weblinks
Gain additional information for research

Slideshows
View images and captions

Try This!
Complete activities and hands-on experiments

Key Words
Study vocabulary, and complete a matching word activity

Quizzes
Test your knowledge

Share
Share titles within your Learning Management System (LMS) or Library Circulation System

Citation
Create bibliographical references following the Chicago Manual of Style

This title is part of our AV2 digital subscription

1-Year 3–8 Subscription
ISBN 978-1-7911-3306-1

Access hundreds of AV2 titles with our digital subscription.
Sign up for a FREE trial at **www.av2books.com/trial**

SEA SNAKES

CONTENTS

Snakes in the Water

Sea snakes are the most **diverse** reptiles in the oceans. There are about 70 different **species** of sea snake. That is 10 times the amount of sea turtle species. Sea snakes are known for their powerful **venom**. These snakes are part of the elapid **family**. This family includes other well-known venomous snakes, such as cobras and coral snakes.

Like all reptiles, sea snakes breathe air and have bony plates, or scales, covering their bodies. They must use their surroundings to warm up or cool down.

SNAKE BITES

Sea snakes can dive up to **800 feet** (250 meters) under the water.

Some sea snakes can **hold their breath** for **8 hours**.

What Do Sea Snakes Look Like?

Sea snakes have thin, flattened bodies and a flat tail. Most sea snakes are 3 to 5 feet (0.9 m to 1.5 m) long, but some can be as long as 9 feet (2.7 m). People have found **fossils** of ancient sea snakes more than 30 feet (9 m) long.

Measuring Up

Average snake lengths

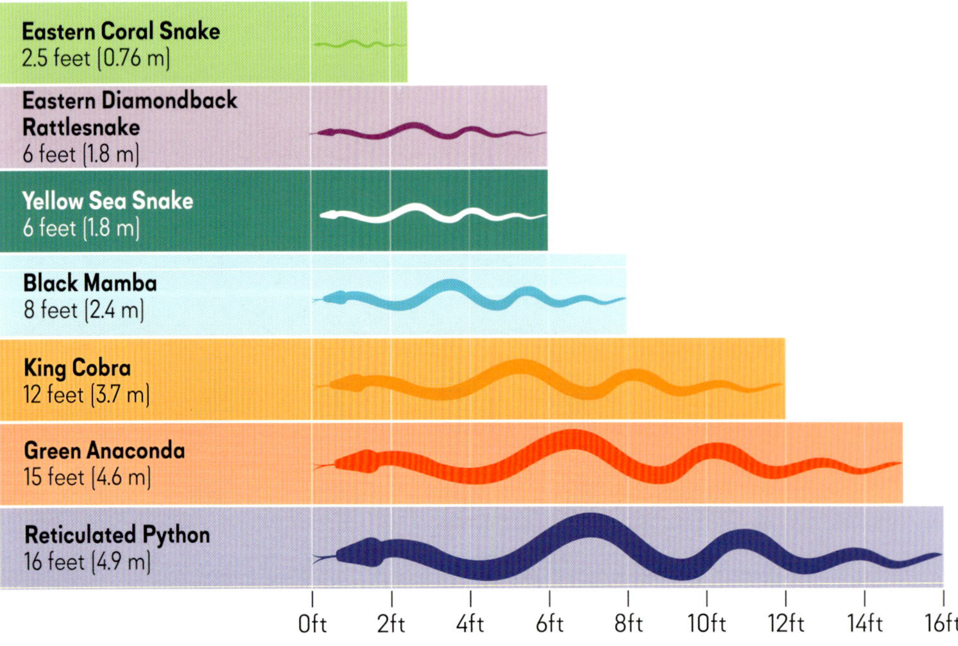

Sea snakes come in many colors. They are often striped with black and white, blue, or gray bands. Some have dramatic markings. For example, the yellow-bellied sea snake is black with a bright yellow belly. A sea snake's bright colors warn **predators** to stay away.

Unlike the scales of snakes that live on land, sea snake scales are typically small and do not overlap. They cannot grip surfaces well. This means most sea snakes cannot slither on land.

The Life Cycle

Like all living things, sea snakes have a life cycle. A sea snake will be born, grow, and **reproduce**. Sea snakes can live up to 10 years.

1

Most sea snakes do not lay eggs. Instead, many female sea snakes keep their eggs inside their bodies, then give birth to live young.

4

Most sea snakes live their entire lives in the ocean. At age two or older, they are ready to find a **mate**. To do this, male sea snakes tap females with their snout.

2
Newborn sea snakes are called neonates. They are born into the ocean or in shallow water. Neonates can swim right after birth.
3
Young sea snakes shed their skin as they grow. They can reach adult size in two years.

A Sea Snake's Body

Like all living things, a sea snake has many different **adaptations**. Some keep the snake safe. Others help it to survive in its **habitat**.

Nose

Sea snakes have nostrils on top of their snouts. This helps them breathe in air without being spotted by flying predators such as eagles.

Salt Gland

Sea snakes have a salt **gland** beneath their tongue that helps remove salt from the ocean that builds up in their bodies.

Lungs
Sea snake lungs run the entire length of the snake's body. They are used to control the snake's **buoyancy**.

Tail
A sea snake's flat tail is used like a paddle when swimming.

Where Sea Snakes Live

North America
Europe
Asia
Africa
South America
Australia
N
W
E
S
Scale
3,000 miles
0
3,000 kilometers
Legend
Indonesia
Mexico
Australia
Land
Water

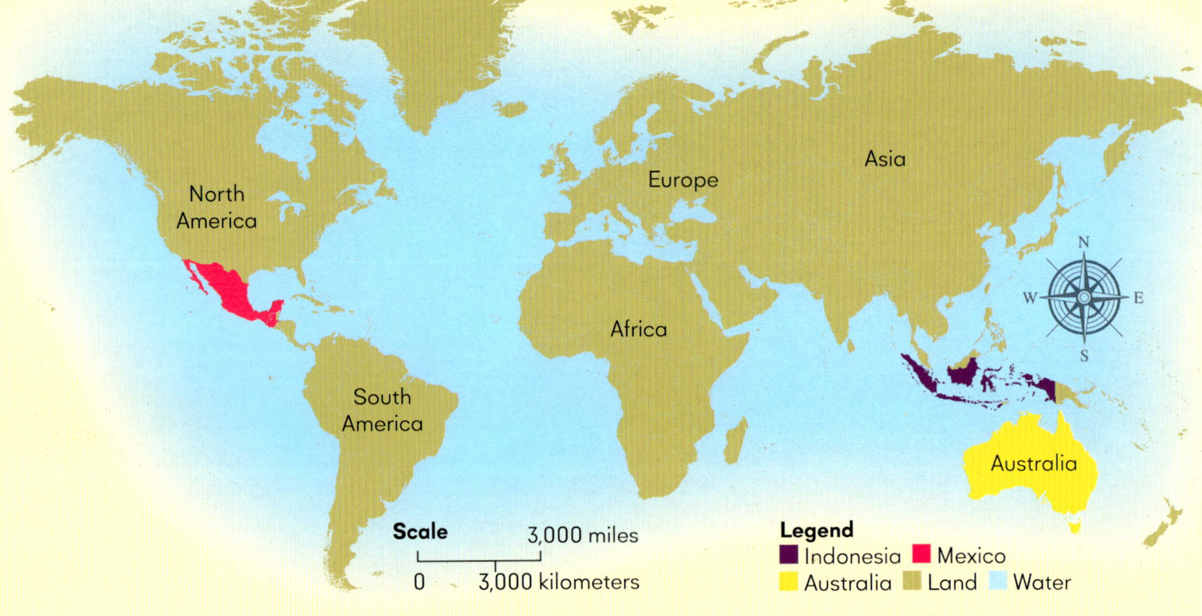

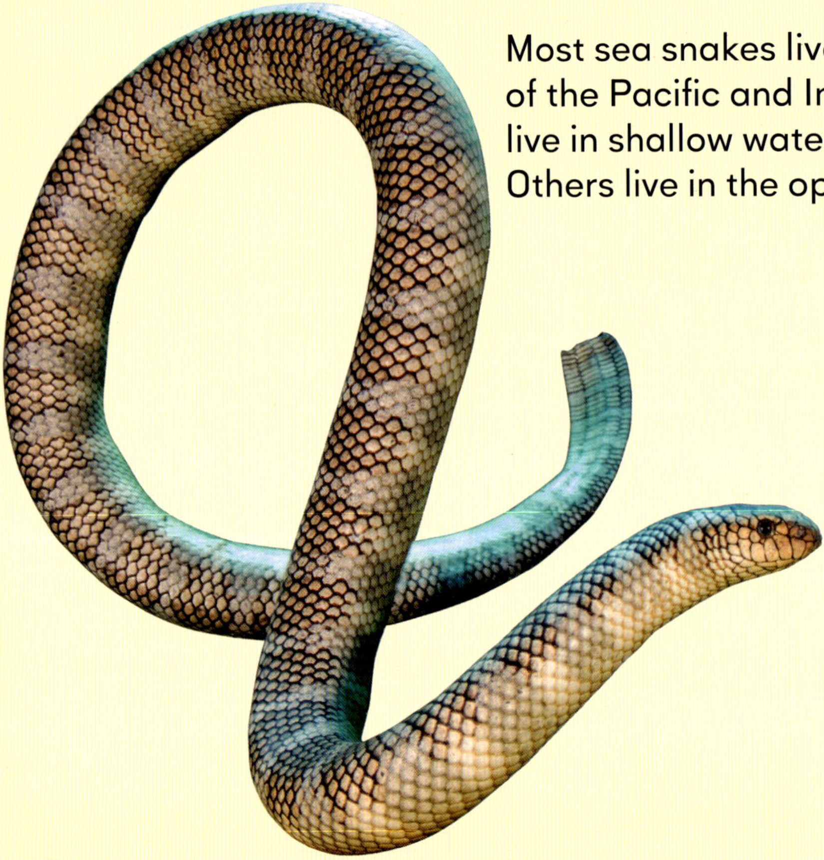

Most sea snakes live in the warm waters of the Pacific and Indian oceans. Many live in shallow waters near coral reefs. Others live in the open ocean.

Sea Snake Range

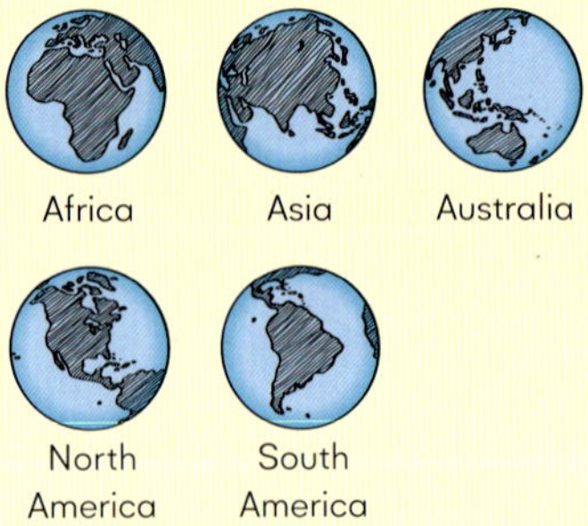

Africa
Asia
Australia
North America
South America

Sea Snake Habitats

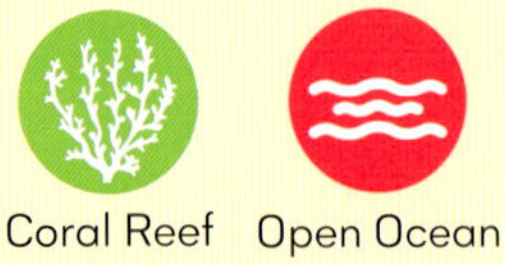

Coral Reef
Open Ocean

Banded Sea Krait

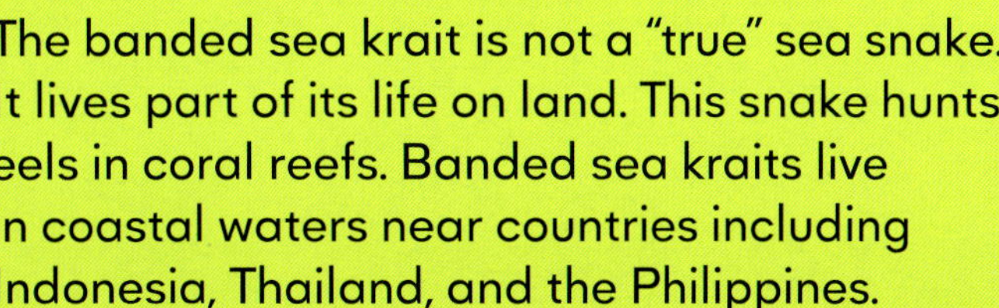

The banded sea krait is not a "true" sea snake. It lives part of its life on land. This snake hunts eels in coral reefs. Banded sea kraits live in coastal waters near countries including Indonesia, Thailand, and the Philippines.

Yellow-Bellied Sea Snake

The yellow-bellied sea snake is unusual because it thrives in the open ocean. It is the most widely ranging snake on Earth and can be found in the ocean near countries including Guatemala, Mexico, Madagascar, Iran, Australia, and China.

Olive Sea Snake

The olive sea snake is one of the most common sea snakes in Australia's coral reefs. It has light sensors in its tail that help it stay completely hidden during the day. At night, it comes out to hunt fish, crabs, and prawns. This snake is curious and sometimes approaches divers.

On the Hunt

Most sea snakes eat fish, although some also eat crabs, fish eggs, and squid. Sea snakes are not fast enough to catch fish in an open chase. Instead, they must be sneaky. Some sea snakes hunt alongside schools of large fish. When the large fish chase small fish into cracks and crevices, the sea snakes dart inside for a meal. They bite their trapped **prey**, paralyze it with venom, and then swallow it whole.

Sea snakes have small fangs, so a person or larger animal may be bitten without noticing.

Some sea snakes, such as turtle-headed sea snakes, only eat fish eggs.

Other sea snakes trick fish. They swim backward or act like a floating stick. When unsuspecting fish come near their open mouth, they quickly turn and strike.

Keeping Safe

Although sea snakes are extremely venomous, they rarely use their venom for defense. They are not typically **aggressive** and prefer to swim away rather than fight. Their bright warning colors are often enough to keep most threats away.

Sharks, such as tiger sharks, and birds, such as sea eagles, prey on sea snakes. Hiding in crevices and keeping most of their body hidden under the water when breathing are two ways sea snakes stay safe.

Sea snakes can get some of the oxygen they need from the water through their skin. This helps them dive for longer.

When sea snakes do bite in self-defense, they often give “blank” or venom-free bites.

Threats to Sea Snakes

Like many animals today, sea snakes face several threats. These include climate change, pollution, and human behavior. Many sea snake populations are **endangered** or **vulnerable**. One major threat to sea snakes is changes in rain. Sea snakes need fresh water to survive but sometimes go months without a drink. They get their water from freshwater rain puddles on top of the ocean's surface. Without reliable rain, sea snakes will be unable to drink.

Unlike other sea snakes, banded sea kraits often leave the ocean to get water from springs or other freshwater sources.

Another threat to sea snakes is hunting. In Asia, hundreds of thousands of sea snakes are hunted each year for food, medicine, and leather. Although a few countries have laws to control sea snake hunting, many others do not. Sometimes, people catch sea snakes when they are fishing. This can lead to dangerous bites.

Deaths from sea snake bites are very rare. Only about 3 percent of these bites are fatal.

Sea snakes are also threatened by pollution. Some sea snakes can absorb **pollutants** into their dark-colored scales. They then shed their skin more often to get rid of the pollutants. This has led scientists to notice that sea snakes in more heavily polluted waters are becoming darker in color.

SNAKE BITES

Sea snakes only have **two to nine young** at a time. This can make it harder for their numbers to recover.

Two sea snake species, the **leaf-scaled sea snake** and the **short-nosed sea snake**, are critically endangered.

ACTIVITY
Create a Sea Snake

There are many different kinds of snakes in the world. They all have certain features in common. However, each snake also has its own unique features. They help the snake live in its home.

Make your own snake by answering the following questions:

1. What is your snake called?
2. Where does it live?
3. What features does it share with other snakes?
4. What features help it live in its home? How do these features do this?
5. What does your snake look like?
6. Use a pencil or pen to draw your snake living in its home. Make sure to include all of its features.

Supplies needed for this activity

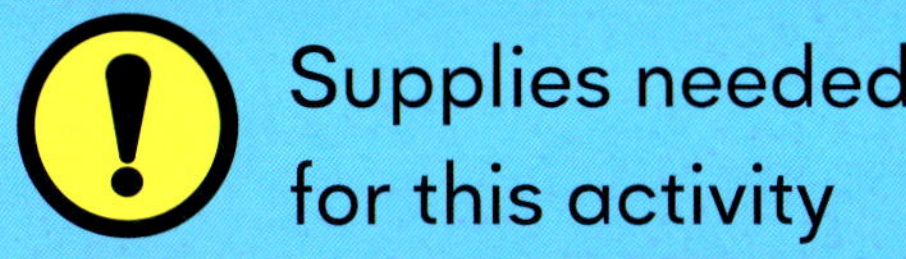

Pencil or pen
Paper
Eraser

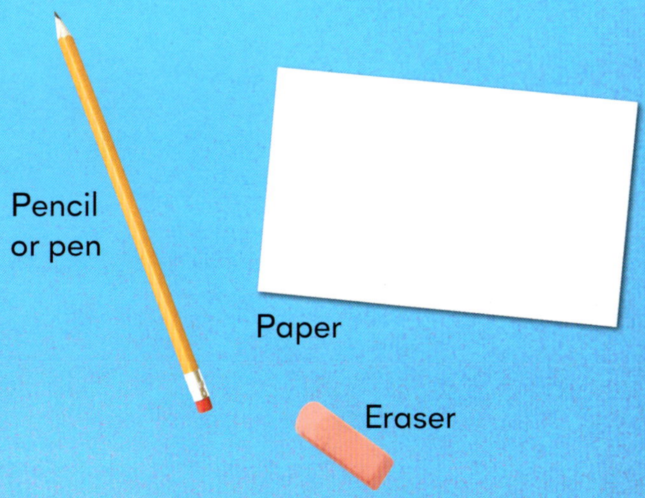

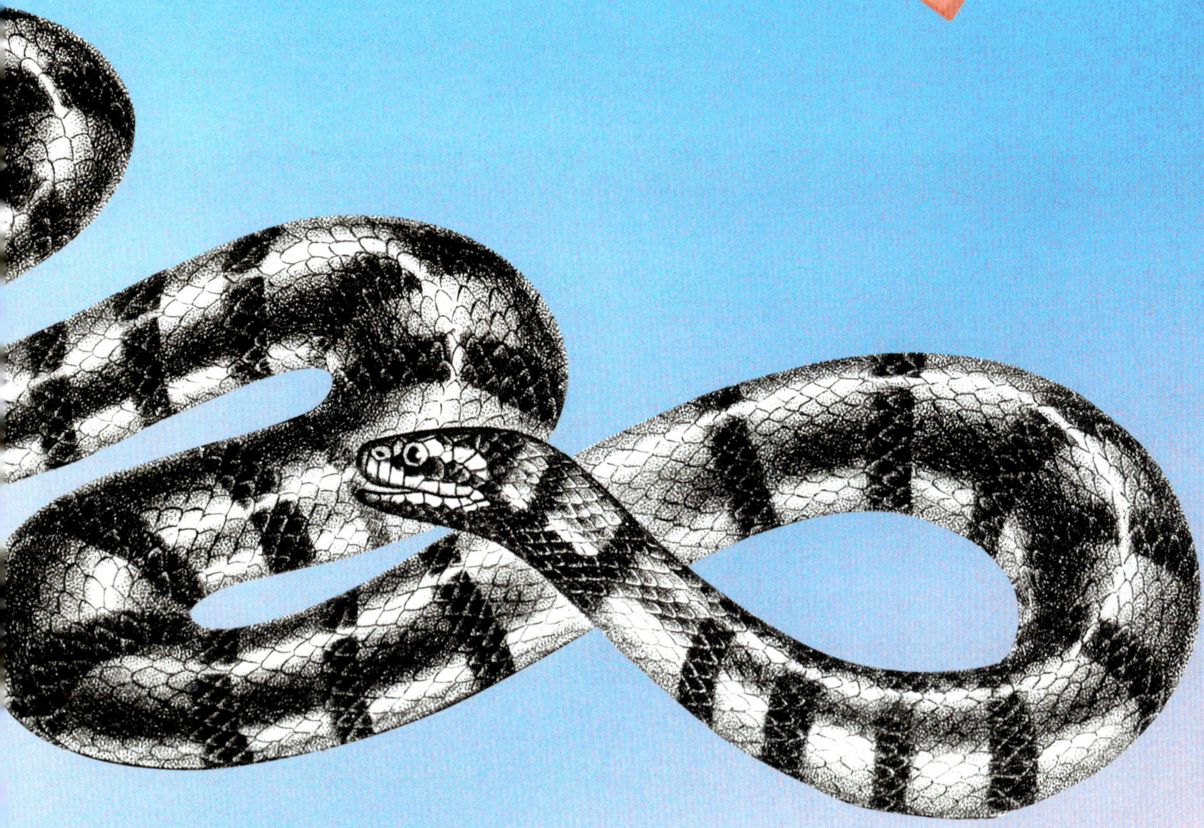

SEA SNAKE QUIZ

How well do you know your sea snakes? Take this short quiz to find out.

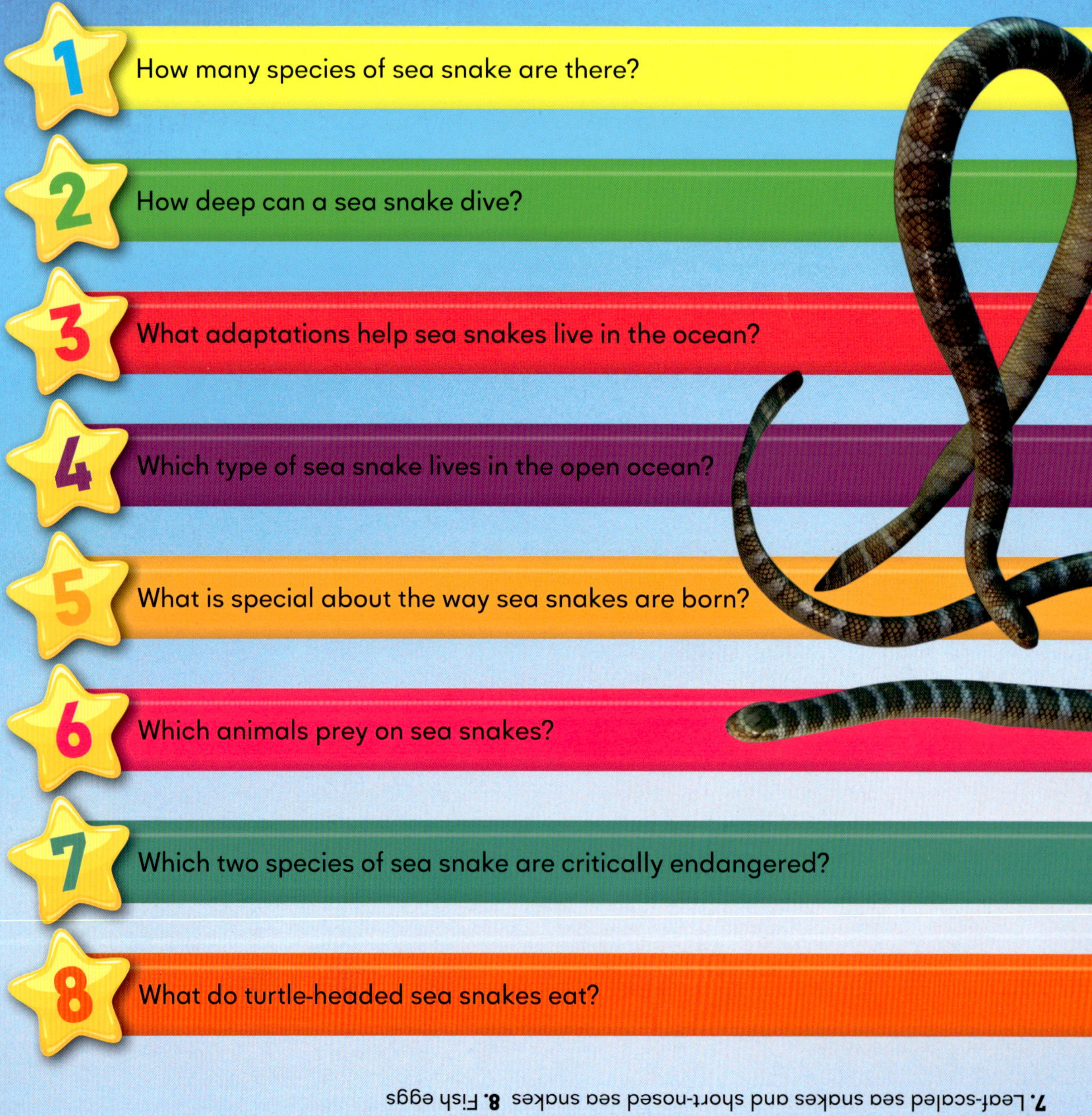

1. How many species of sea snake are there?
2. How deep can a sea snake dive?
3. What adaptations help sea snakes live in the ocean?
4. Which type of sea snake lives in the open ocean?
5. What is special about the way sea snakes are born?
6. Which animals prey on sea snakes?
7. Which two species of sea snake are critically endangered?
8. What do turtle-headed sea snakes eat?

ANSWERS

1. 70 **2.** 800 feet (250 m) **3.** Flat tails, raised nostrils, elongated lungs, and salt glands
4. Yellow-bellied sea snake **5.** The young are born live **6.** Sharks and birds
7. Leaf-scaled sea snakes and short-nosed sea snakes **8.** Fish eggs

Key Words

adaptations: changes in animals or plants that make them better able to survive in their homes

aggressive: ready to fight

buoyancy: the ability to float in air or water

diverse: showing a wide variety

endangered: close to becoming extinct

family: a group of living things that share certain characteristics

fossils: remains of ancient plants or animals

gland: a part of a body that produces substances it can use

habitat: the place where a plant or animal lives

mate: a member of a pair of animals that can reproduce or have babies

pollutants: harmful substances like chemicals or waste

predators: animals that hunt other animals

prey: animals that are hunted by other animals

reproduce: to have babies

species: a group of closely related animals or plants

venom: a toxic chemical produced by some animals

vulnerable: likely to become endangered soon

Index

Published by AV2
276 5th Avenue
Suite 704 #917
New York, NY 10001
Website: www.av2books.com

Library of Congress Control Number: 2021940102

ISBN 978-1-7911-4151-6 (hardcover)
ISBN 978-1-7911-4152-3 (softcover)
ISBN 978-1-7911-4153-0 (multi-user eBook)

Printed in Guangzhou, China
1 2 3 4 5 6 7 8 9 0 25 24 23 22 21

062021
101120

Art Director: Terry Paulhus Project Coordinator: John Willis

Every reasonable effort has been made to trace ownership and to obtain permission to reprint copyright material. The publisher would be pleased to have any errors or omissions brought to its attention so that they may be corrected in subsequent printings.

The publisher acknowledges Alamy, Getty Images, Minden Pictures, and Shutterstock as the primary image suppliers for this title.